The Lonely Lobster

WRITTEN BY BETH COSTANZO

ILLUSTRATED BY ERIC D. ERWIN

www.adventuresofscubajack.com

Copyright 2018 by The Adventures of Scuba Jack, Inc.
All Rights Reserved.

Dedication:

"This book is dedicated to all those friends near and dear to my heart"

There once was a little lobster

as lonely as can be.

He lived upon the sandy floor

at the bottom of the sea.

The little lobster lived alone

and this really made him blue.

All he wanted was a friend

to show his treasure to.

One stormy day a wave came in,

and when the bubbles cleared

There on the sand next to him

a tiny crab appeared.

"Hello there!" said the Lobster.

"I am glad you came to play.

I was just about to have some lunch.

Would you like to stay?"

"I would love to!" said the crab.

"I've been hungry for a while.

You asking me to share your lunch

has really made me smile!"

After lunch the two just talked about the fun they had.
Since the lobster met the crab he was no longer sad.

The two remained the best of friends having adventures every day. They explored nearby shipwrecks and found new games to play.

The little lobster and the crab

were happy as can be.

They couldn't think of a nicer place

than underneath the sea.

www.adventuresofscubajack.com

www.ingramcontent.com/pod-product-compliance
Lightning Source LLC
LaVergne TN
LVRC091352060526
838200LV00035B/499